JOURNEY INTO CIVILIZATION
ANCIENT GREECE

by Robert Nicholson

CHELSEA JUNIORS
A division of Chelsea House Publishers
New York • Philadelphia

Editorial Consultant: Patsy Banags, British Museum, London

This edition published 1994 by Chelsea House Publishers, a division of Main Line Book Co.
300 Park Avenue South, New York, N.Y. 10010 by arrangement with Two-Can Publishing Ltd.
This edition copyright © Two-Can Publishing Ltd., 1994

First published in Great Britain in 1992 by Two-Can Publishing Ltd., 346 Old Street, London EC1V 9NQ
Original edition © Two-Can Publishing Ltd 1992
All rights reserved.

3 5 7 9 8 6 4 2

ISBN 0-7910-2703-1
ISBN 0-7910-2727-9 (pbk.)

Printed in Hong Kong by Wing King Tong Co. Ltd.

Photographic credits:
Ancient Art and Architecture Collection: p9(r), p10, p11(b), p16, p19(t);
The Bridgeman Art Library: p22(t), p23(b); ET Archive: p13(t), p30(l);
Werner Forman: p7; Michael Holford: p9(t,c), p11, p15, p19(b), p20,
p22(l), p23(t), p24, p30(t); Toby: p20(b), Zefa: p30(b)

Illustration credits:
Maxine Hamil: cover, p25-29; Mike Allport p3-24

Contents

All words that appear in **bold** can be found in the glossary.

Macedonia

A D R I A T I C   S E A

Pindus Mountains

Italy

Troy

Mt Olympus

A E G E A N

Delphi

Athens

Peloponnesus

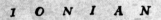

Olympia

Sparta

I O N I A N

S E A

S E A   O F
C R E T E

The Greek World

The civilization of ancient Greece lasted
from about 2000 B.C. to 200 B.C. The peak
came during what is called the classical
period, between 500 B.C and 400 B.C. At this
time, Greeks controlled the mainland and
the islands we now know as Greece, as well
as the land around the eastern end of the
Mediterranean, which was settled by Greek
traders and farmers.

During this time the Greek people lived
in many separate city-states. Each city-state
was based around one city and included
the surrounding countryside. Greek thinkers
and artists wanted to make these just and
beautiful places to live. Many of their ideas
and inventions influenced Europe and its
peoples as they developed. From there,
Greek ideals have spread all over the world.

Crete

Home of Minotaur

M E D I T E R R A

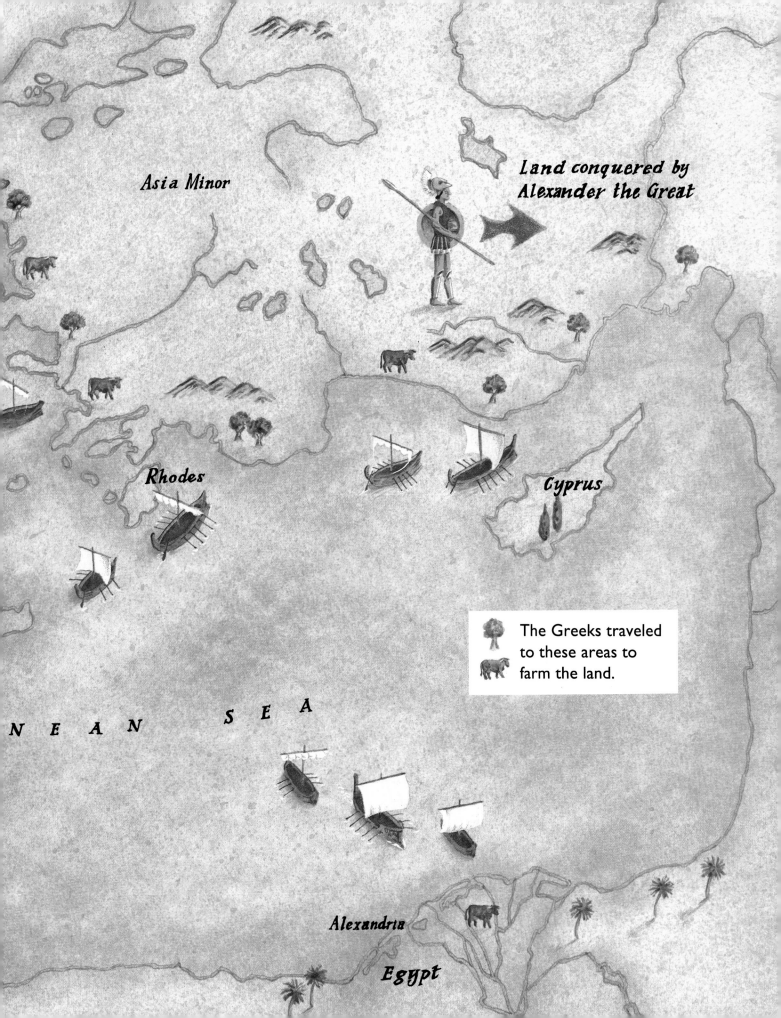

Asia Minor

Land conquered by
Alexander the Great

Rhodes

Cyprus

The Greeks traveled
to these areas to
farm the land.

N E A N   S E A

Alexandria

Egypt

Greek Lands

Mainland Greece and the islands that surround it are hot and dry with many high mountains and steep-sided valleys. Its hills and valleys were once heavily wooded, but by the classical period many of the forests had been cut down. The Greek mainland is surrounded almost entirely by water.

Because the countryside was so rugged, the ancient Greeks had to farm near the coast and in sheltered valleys. Their most important crops were wheat, barley, grapes and olives. However, the Greeks were skilled sailors and keen traders, which meant that they could import food.

Small village communities were very isolated from one another because of the high mountains and steep valleys. There were very few roads, and most journeys had to be made on foot.

▲ Because travel over land was so difficult, the Greeks traveled by sea whenever possible. Stormy seas and rugged coasts meant that this could be very dangerous. Sailors had no compasses and had to navigate by the stars.

▶ Olive trees growing on a dry, rocky hillside.

City-States

Ancient Greece was not one united country, but instead was made up of separate city-states. A city-state, or **polis**, was based around one city and included all the surrounding farms, villages and houses.

Athens was the city of education and learning. Athenian philosophers, politicians and artists were famous throughout Greece. About 300,000 people lived in the city itself and the surrounding countryside.

The city of Sparta was Athens's greatest rival and was famous for the strength of its army. There were many wars between the two cities as each tried to gain control of the whole of Greece.

▼ This is the ancient city of Athens. The acropolis, which means "high city," was easy to defend in times of war. The main temple of the city, the Parthenon, was built on this hill.

The Peloponnesian War

The rivalry between Athens and Sparta eventually led to the Peloponnesian War (431 to 404 B.C.). Sparta attacked Athens first, fearful of the city's growing power. After many triumphs and setbacks, Sparta won the war, but both states were weakened after 27 years of fighting.

▶ Their only defense was their bronze shields.

▲ This vase painting shows Greek soldiers armed with shields, spears and swords.

▲ Greek soldiers used a variety of weapons: spears, javelins, daggers, arrows and slingshots.

Citizens and Slaves

In Greek cities, there were groups of people with different rights and different roles to play in society. **Citizens** were the most important and had the most rights. They could own property and take part in politics and the law.

In Athens and some other cities, most male adults were citizens. Women, **slaves** and foreigners were not. In Sparta, far fewer were citizens. Only men from the richest families had citizen's rights, which meant only one in ten adult men.

Slaves were usually captured prisoners of war. They were owned by the people they worked for and were bought and sold like property. Some lived comfortably with the families who owned them. Others lived in miserable conditions or worked in mines until they died. Most slaves were paid for much of the work they did. If they saved enough money, they could buy their freedom.

▲ Each Greek city minted its own coins, stamped with the city symbol such as the owl of Athens.

▲ This vase painting shows women slaves drawing water from a fountain.

Government

Many of the city-states of ancient Greece were **democracies**. In a democracy, the decisions about government are made by councils of ordinary citizens. Only adult men were entitled to be citizens. Some city-states, however, were ruled by rich and powerful landowners, supported by armies.

In Athens, all citizens voted to decide how the city was run, what taxes to pay, whether to go to war and so on. Poor workers were even paid a full day's wages to attend the government assemblies. There were no separate politicians or lawyers in Athens. All citizens took part in politics and legal affairs.

▲ Men on juries used disks such as these to vote in courts of law. Hollow disks indicated "guilty," solid "not guilty."

▲ Citizens could vote to banish politicians by writing their names on these pottery fragments, called **ostraka**.

Philosophers and Scientists

The ancient Greeks were very curious about themselves and the world around them and made many important advances in science, learning and art. Great thinkers were known as **philosophers** no matter what subject they studied. The word philosophy comes from the Greek words for "love of wisdom." Philosophers tried to find out how the universe worked, why people were good or evil, and how people should live their lives.

Many Greek discoveries provide the foundations of our knowledge and beliefs.

Greeks studied the stars and discovered that the earth floated freely in space, turning on its own axis. They also correctly predicted eclipses of the sun. Sometimes they were wrong. Ptolemy, a Greek scholar, thought the earth was the center of the universe.

Most new ideas were never used for solving practical problems. Metal-working techniques, for example, were still primitive and never developed enough to make tools that could take advantage of the advances made in science.

Famous Philosophers

● **Hippocrates** (about 460 – 377 B.C.)
Hippocrates founded a medical school, where he practiced scientific medicine instead of magic or religion. He taught the value of knowing how the body worked.

● **Aristotle** (384 – 322 B.C.)
Aristotle examined living things in nature. He also wrote on many subjects, including politics, and invented a method of thinking called logic.

● **Socrates** (about 469 – 399 B.C.)
Socrates, one of the first great philosophers of classical Greece, taught the value of questioning common beliefs in order to find new ideas and explore new truths.

▲ Bust of Socrates

● **Plato** (about 427 – 347 B.C.)
Plato founded a school for philosophers called the Academy. He taught Aristotle there. His famous books are *The Republic* and *Dialogues*.

◄ The Greek philosopher Eratosthenes calculated the circumference of the earth by measuring the angle of the sun at Alexandria in northern Egypt, and measuring the distance from there to Syene in southern Egypt, where the sun was overhead at noon. His figure for the circumference was correct to within nearly 200 miles.

13

Soothsayers and Oracles

The Greeks had many gods and goddesses. They usually represented a particular aspect of life, such as love or war. Most of them were believed to live on **Mount Olympus**. The Greeks told stories about their gods, in which they fought and loved and were angry or jealous just like men and women.

Many of the gods had temples where priests or priestesses performed rituals in their honor. Gods were often honored by **sacrifices**. Usually these were just gifts of food and wine, but on big feast days or festivals, many animals were sacrificed.

The Greeks looked to the gods for answers to all their problems. For simple questions, such as "Should I marry this man?" they would go to a **soothsayer**. He or she would study the weather or the insides of a sacrificed animal to find the gods' answer.

For more complicated questions, such as "How should we defeat our enemies?" a visit to an **oracle** was necessary. At Delphi, the famous oracle, a priestess called Pythia would go into a trance and give a reply that had to be interpreted by priests. It cost a lot of money to consult Pythia.

The Olympic Games

The Greeks believed that having a physically fit body was a way of honoring the gods. Games were held all over Greece in honor of different gods or festivals. The Olympic Games were held once every four years in honor of Zeus. They lasted five days, and people came from all over Greece to compete in athletic events. Wars were even postponed for three months so that people could travel safely to see the games. The events included boxing, wrestling, discus throwing, javelin throwing, long jumping, running and chariot races.

Important gods

ZEUS and **HERA** were the king and queen of the gods.

POSEIDON was the brother of Zeus and the god of the sea.

DIONYSUS was the god of wine.

ARES was the god of war.

HERMES was the messenger god.

APOLLO was the god of music and healing.

▲ Aphrodite, the goddess of love

◄ Athena, the goddess of wisdom and of Athens itself, is born from the head of Zeus.

Theater and Writing

Even today, ancient Greek literature is still read and plays are still performed.

Poetry was the earliest form of Greek literature. Homer was the first major poet. He wrote long poems telling the stories of the adventures of heroes and gods. His best-known poems are the *Iliad* and the *Odyssey*.

The Greeks were the first civilization to record their history as it happened. Before this, people passed on the news of events by word of mouth and their stories quickly became exaggerated.

▲ In comedies, costumes were padded, making the actors look grotesquely funny.

Drama

Drama developed from songs and dances to honor the gods. Theaters were built next to temples, and plays were an important part of religious festivals. There were two sorts of plays: tragedies and comedies.

Tragedies were sad and violent tales of love and war. They often retold old myths about the gods and related them to the lives of people. Comedies made fun of politics, religion and important local people.

▶ Greek actors always wore masks, which depicted different facial expressions and moods. Wide mouths made it easier for them to project their voices.

At Home

Most Greeks were farmers or craftsmen living in simple houses. Businesses were family run with a few slaves to help out.

Greek houses were arranged around a courtyard with an altar in the middle. Ordinary Greek houses were made from mud bricks dried in the sun. It was easy to dig through the walls, so burglars were known as wall diggers.

▶ Parts of this house have been cut away so you can see inside.

The living rooms were on the ground floor, with bedrooms above. Often men and women had separate living areas and spent most of their time apart. Food was cooked over open fires in the kitchen. The smoke escaped through a hole in the roof.

kitchen

altar

living room

herm

▶ Inside a typical Greek house, walls were plain with just a few hangings. Chests were used for storage.

Clothes

Men's tunics were made from wool or linen. A plain square of material called a **chiton** was fastened over one or both shoulders and belted around the waist. Women wore a long tunic called a **peplos** or a long chiton. Wealthier people had tunics made from decorated material, while slaves had plain tunics. In classical times, it was fashionable for men to have short hair and a beard.

Cloaks and shawls would be worn outside in colder weather and for traveling. Many people went barefoot most of the time. Shoes were leather sandals or boots.

Although Greek cities always had public baths, there was no soap, so the Greeks rubbed their bodies with olive oil to get clean. Then they would scrape the oil and dirt off with a tool called a **strigil**.

▼ A gold necklace like the one worn by the woman in the vase painting below.

bathroom

well

▶ A seated woman is adorned with jewelry for her wedding. She wears a chiton sewn up on both sides to cover her arms.

◀ At the front of most houses stood a statue of the god Hermes – a **herm** – thought to act as a guard for the house.

19

Food

The ancient Greek diet was simple and very healthy. The Greeks ate bread, cheese, fruit, vegetables, eggs and very little meat. Only wealthy people could afford to eat meat often. Many Greeks lived near the sea, so fish and seafood were very popular.

Farmers grew wheat, barley, grapes and olives. Grapes were eaten or made into wine. Olives were pressed for their oil, which was used for cooking, lighting and cleaning. Some farmers kept animals such as pigs, sheep and goats. Bees were kept for honey. Vegetables such as peas, beans, turnips, garlic and onions were also grown, as well as fruit such as pomegranates, dates, figs and melons.

Breakfast and lunch were small meals, and the main meal was in the evening. Often the Greeks held big dinner parties. Only men were invited, and they would sit on couches, eating several courses and drinking lots of wine. After the meal, the men would stay to drink and have a discussion at a **symposium**, or drinking party.

▲ This vase painting shows the messenger of the gods bringing mankind the gift of corn.

figs

pomegranates

fresh dates

olives

dried dates

Greek Sweetmeats

The Greeks ate **sweetmeats** – made from dates, figs, nuts, sesame seeds and honey – between courses at a symposium, or as little snacks. Here are some for you to make.

Put 3$\frac{1}{2}$ ounces of sesame seeds into a saucepan with 4 large tablespoons of honey. Ask an adult to help you simmer the mixture over low heat for 10-20 minutes, until it is a rich golden color. You can tell if it is ready by dropping a spoonful on a wet plate, letting it cool, then working it into a ball. If it keeps its shape, it is ready. Take the pan off the heat and stir the mixture every few minutes until it is almost cold. Wet your hands with cold water and roll spoonfuls of the mixture into 20 to 25 little balls. Wrap each sweetmeat in waxed paper.

grapes

Arts and Crafts

The Greeks thought that there was a perfect shape for any object, whether it was a simple clay pot or a huge temple. They used both mathematics and ideas about what is good in art, known as **aesthetics,** to try to make their art as beautiful as possible.

▲ The Greeks made elegant pots covered in patterns and paintings. Many were used every day for storing water, oil or wine, but some of the most beautiful pots were kept and then buried with the dead.

◀ Greek statues were made from stone or bronze. Early statues were not lifelike, but as the skills of sculptors developed, the statues became graceful, with expressive faces and clothes that look real. Most stone statues were painted, but have now lost their color.

► The Parthenon in Athens is one of the finest Greek buildings still standing. It is made from carved blocks of cream-colored marble and held together with wooden pegs and metal clamps. Each side is decorated with rows of columns, typical of Greek architecture. This classical style has been copied all over the world. Is there a building like this near where you live?

Bronze Statues

Bronze statues were made using the "lost wax" method.

▼ When the clay was finally removed, a bronze statue was revealed.

First, a clay model was made and wooden pegs were stuck into it. Then the clay model was covered with a thin layer of wax. The details of the statue's face and clothes were then sculpted onto the wax.

The model was covered with clay and heated so the wax melted and ran out. Molten bronze was poured between the layers of clay.

Growing Up

Greek boys went to school from the age of 7 until they were 15. Fees were charged, so usually boys from poorer families did not stay at school long. Girls were taught to cook and look after the house by their mothers.

In Athens and many other cities, boys learned reading, writing and math, as well as music, poetry and sports.

In Sparta, life was much harder. If babies were weak or ill, they were left to die on the hillside. Boys were taught to be tough to prepare them for their life as soldiers. At the age of seven, they were sent away to a strict boarding school. They had no sandals or warm clothes and had to sleep on the hard ground. They were left hungry and had to steal and hunt for their own food. They were beaten and taught to fight and use soldiers' weapons.

◀ This baby's bottle would have been fitted with a leather or cloth nipple.

▶ A child's terra-cotta doll, with jointed arms and legs.

The Greek Alphabet

Some Greek letters are similar to those we use today. You may have heard some of their names before. Do you know where our word "alphabet" comes from?

Greek letter	Name	English sound		Greek letter	Name	English sound		Greek letter	Name	English sound		Greek letter	Name	English sound
A α	alpha	a		H η	eta	ey		N ν	nu	n		T τ	tau	t
B β	beta	b		Θ θ	theta	th		Ξ ξ	xi	ks		Y υ	upsilon	u
Γ γ	gamma	g		I ι	iota	i		O o	omicron	o		Φ φ	phi	ph
Δ δ	delta	d		K κ	kappa	k		Π π	pi	p		X χ	chi	ch
E ε	epsilon	e		Λ λ	lambda	l		P ρ	rho	r		Ψ ψ	psi	ps
Z ζ	zeta	z		M μ	mu	m		Σ σ,ς	sigma	s		Ω ω	omega	oh

Theseus and the Minotaur

The ancient Greeks told many tales, or myths, about their gods and about the world around them. Myths often included real events from Greek history. This tale recalls a time long ago when Greece was dominated by the island of Crete, and Athens was not yet a powerful city-state. It tells the story of the hero Theseus, who overcame the Minotaur, a terrifying beast that was half man and half bull.

Athenians trembled at the very mention of Crete. The name Minotaur was enough to make the bravest man shiver. Every nine years, King Minos of Crete demanded a terrible tribute from the Athenians. Seven young men and seven young women were sent to Crete to be fed to the fearsome Minotaur. A ship with black sails would come to Athens each time the tribute was due. As the ship sailed, a huge crowd would gather at the harbor, weeping and wailing.

In Crete, the prisoners were guests of honor at a huge banquet. They were given fine clothes, and offered the most delicious food. Few of them could eat. Afterward, they were shut in a large room filled with every possible luxury, but few could sleep.

The next day, they were taken to some wooden doors, carved with pictures of galloping bulls. From behind the doors came a loud bellowing and stamping. The doors opened and a prisoner was pushed through.

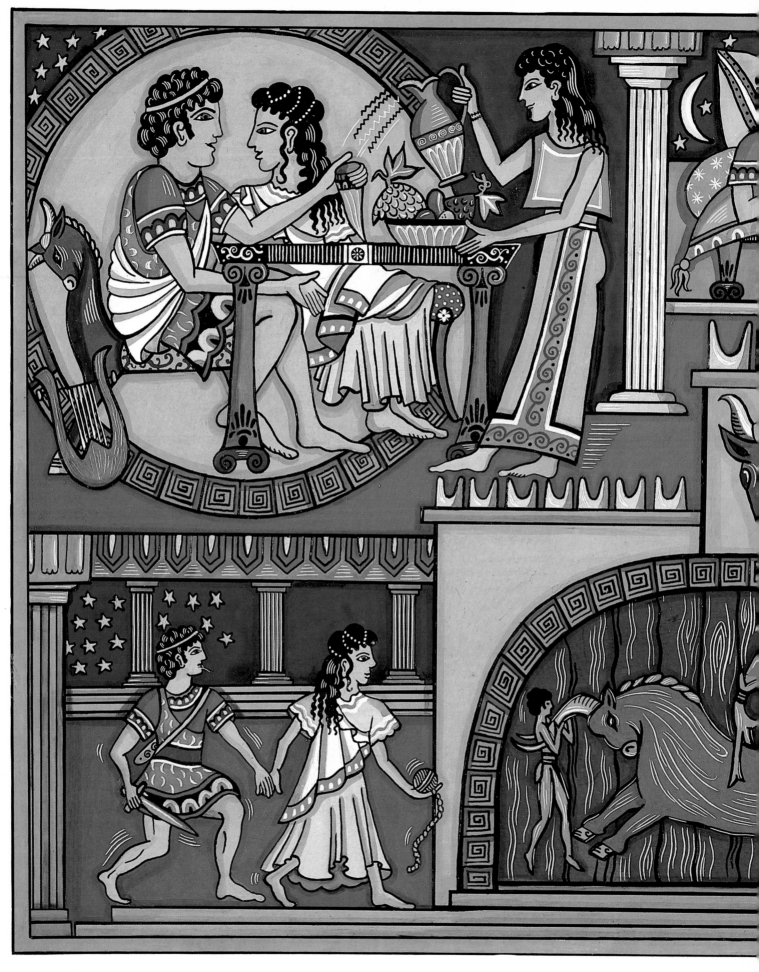

The small crowd of prisoners, guards and priestesses waited until they heard a blood-curdling scream. Then a priestess would point to the next prisoner to be sent through the doors. This went on until the prisoners had all met their fate. Then the Athenians could rest easy for nine years, until it was time to make another tribute.

One year, young Theseus was among the people sent as tribute to Crete. He, unlike the other prisoners, sat dry-eyed on the ship. He laughed and chatted as they prepared for the banquet, until the others began to feel quite cheerful, too. At the banquet, he sat near King Minos's daughter Ariadne, who was charmed by this handsome and brave young man. All evening, they sat and talked.

Ariadne told Theseus that behind the doors there was an elaborate maze. Innumerable paths twisted and turned, confusing the eye and the mind. A person entering the maze could never find his way out.

In the very heart of the maze lived the Minotaur. He knew all the twists and turns and blind alleys. If someone stumbled into the maze, the Minotaur would find him or her within moments.

Ariadne was determined to help the brave Theseus. After the banquet, she crept into the sleeping chamber and called softly to Theseus. All his weapons had been taken away, but Ariadne handed him a sword. Then she led the way to the great carved wooden door of the maze.

"Here I must wait for you," she said, and she handed Theseus a ball of thread.

"What is this for?" Theseus said, puzzled.

"As you walk through the maze, unwind this thread behind you. If you succeed, you can follow the thread back. The Minotaur will be asleep, so creep silently through the passages until you reach his lair. With surprise on your side, you may beat him."

Theseus took the thread from Ariadne and pushed open the great door. He stepped inside and closed the door, trapping the end of the thread in the crack. Then, holding his sword in front of him, Theseus headed into the puzzling maze. He could hear the snores of the Minotaur, and set off toward the noise. A few minutes later, however, he could hardly hear the noise. The path had doubled back, and he was now farther away from the center than when he had started. Theseus picked up the hanging thread and followed it back to the last place where there had been a choice of paths.

"If I take a path that seems to lead toward the Minotaur, I end up farther away," he said to himself. "So, if I choose a path that leads away, I will eventually reach the Minotaur."

So Theseus set off, creeping quietly along a path that appeared to lead away from the Minotaur's snores. Suddenly, he found himself stumbling into the mouth of a dark cave. From inside, he heard a huge roar followed by the sound of heavy footsteps. The Minotaur appeared at the entrance.

Theseus gasped. The Minotaur was even more terrifying than he had imagined.

It had the body of a huge, strong man, and the head of an angry bull. Theseus picked up his sword, which he had dropped when he stumbled, just as the Minotaur leapt forward to grab him. He struck a mighty blow to the Minotaur's leg. The Minotaur was not used to people fighting back. Most of his victims were prisoners who were resigned to their fate and did not resist. Within a few minutes, Theseus had killed the Minotaur with a few skillful jabs of his sword.

Picking up the end of Ariadne's thread, he retraced his steps through the maze to the outer door. Ariadne was waiting for him.

"Quick," she whispered, "we must hurry. Once my father finds out, he will send all the guards to look for us."

Theseus and Ariadne hurried back to the room where the prisoners were held and told them what had happened. Ariadne distracted the guard while the prisoners slipped out. Then she led them all down to the harbor. They set sail for Athens just as the alarm was raised in the palace.

Theseus was proclaimed a hero by the people of Athens. The Athenians rejoiced that they no longer had to pay their terrible tribute to King Minos.

How We Know

Have you ever wondered how we know so much about the ancient Greeks when they lived so many hundreds of years ago?

Evidence from the Ground

The Greeks built many buildings and made many beautiful objects. Many of these survive but are buried underground. As archaeologists dig them up, they learn more and more about Greek civilization. Pictures on pottery, for example, often represent scenes from real life.

▲ The painting that decorates this plate shows two Greek heroes fighting over the body of a soldier.

Evidence Around Us

Many Greek buildings still stand today as evidence of the skill of Greek builders and architects. Most European languages have words that were originally Greek, especially words connected with the arts, such as *drama*, and scientific words like *psychology* and *astronomy*.

▲ Alexander the Great in a detail from a Roman mosaic showing his battle against the Persian Emperor, Darius. Alexander extended Greek territory as far east as India. He brought Greek ideas and customs to all the countries he conquered.

Evidence from Books

The Greeks kept records of all sorts of things, from history and philosophy to lists of goods in stores. Many of these survive, and they tell us all about the Greeks and their lives.

▲ The Theseus temple still stands in Athens.

Glossary

aesthetics
Ideas about what is good in art. The Greeks believed that balance and symmetry were very important in art.

chiton
A simple tunic worn by men and women.

citizen
A man who had the right to own property and take part in politics and law.

democracy
A political system based on government by the citizens. In Greece, only men with property were entitled to be citizens with the right to vote on matters of government.

herm
A small statue of the god Hermes, which was placed in front of the house to protect it.

Mount Olympus
The mountain in Greece where the gods were thought to have lived.

oracle
A holy place where the gods could be asked questions with the help of a priest or priestess.

ostraka
A pottery fragment on which citizens wrote the names of the politicians they wished to banish from the city.

peplos
A long tunic worn by women only.

philosopher
A person who seeks wisdom and enlightenment through study and reasoning

polis
A state consisting of a city and the surrounding countryside.

sacrifice
An offering made to a god to bring good fortune or to ask the god not to be angry.

slave
A worker who was owned by a citizen. Slaves had few rights, but they could buy their freedom if they saved enough money.

strigil
A curved blade, usually of metal, used for scraping oil and dirt from the skin.

soothsayer
A person who could predict the future and tell fortunes.

sweetmeats
A small sweet snack often made from preserved fruit or nuts.

symposium
A drinking party where discussions were held, and entertainments may have taken place.

31

Index